# Young Jesus Chronicles

By Spencer Smith and Mark Penta

Spencer would like to thank:
Everyone who has endured listening to him
talk about this book over the last 10 years,
as if it was actually going to happen.
(Especially Mom & family)

Mark would like to thank:
Spencer, for his great sense of humor,
and Jesus, who he prays has one.

They both thank:
Joanne, Cliff, & Jessica

# Introduction

For centuries, readers of The New Testament were left to speculate about Jesus' childhood.

Recently, archeologists made a startling discovery, unearthing what theologians and historians alike have hailed as "the definitive account of the life and times of a boy named Jesus."

Due to the significance of this unprecedented finding, the Vatican called upon the world's foremost experts to decipher these time-ravaged documents...

# 0 - VI A.D.

"Frankincense and myrrh?...I thought we all agreed on the Diaper Genie."

The Manger Maternity Ward

The First Supper

"The least you could do is change a diaper once in a while!"

"Mary! How come I never see you anymore?
You used to be my best customer!"

First steps.

The Sippy Cup of Christ

"He gets it from his Father's side."

The 'H' revealed.

# VII - XII A.D.

The Sermon at the Jungle Gym

Jesus saves.

Jesus spends.

"Now Jesus...God given talent isn't enough.
You need to practice, practice, practice!"

Sweet Jesus.

Father's Day

Before he was tempted by the devil in the desert,
Jesus was tempted by the Devil's Food Cake dessert.

"Oh sure, you can turn water into wine. Let's see you turn fat into muscle, chubby!"

Holy roller.

"I don't care what all the other kids are wearing.
Now put this on!"

"Dad bless you."

Hide and Seek

"Matthew, Mark, Luke, and John, see me after class.
Your book reports are surprisingly similar."

'Stairway to Heaven' was always the last song at the
Nazareth Middle School dances.

"Give us this day your daily lunch money!"

Jesus' first encounter with Judas.

Spin the Goblet.

The original Soccer Mom.

...And when He was hungry, she gave Him meat ravioli with tater tots.

Lesser Known Miracle #1: The Raising of The Frogs

"I suspect a little help from Dad on this one."

# XIII - XVIII A.D.

"You can't tell me what to do! You're not my Father!"

Chariot Driver's Ed

"It's like my father is living vicariously through me.
It's always his dreams, his goals, regardless of what I want.
Aw, but you wouldn't understand, would you Jesus?"

In the high school talent show, nobody wanted to follow Jesus.

"This is only a learner's permit, son. It requires you to have a parent in the vehicle with you at all times."

"Alright boys, you know the drill. Three seconds left, down by one...get the ball to Jesus."

"As your Guidance Counselor, I suggest you rethink your chosen fields. I don't see a future for you in either 'public speaking' or 'saving mankind'."

He could cure the blind, but He couldn't cure the blonde.

"It was a great team effort, but we couldn't have won without
the help of Our Lord and Savior, Jesus Christ."

"Don't worry about the runner...He shalt not steal."

Lesser Known Miracle #2: Jesus cures chronic acne in local youth.

Despite his best efforts, Jesus could not create a miracle
when it came to Irvin M. Knucklebaum.

"I'll see you...and raise myself from the dead."

# About the Scribes

Spencer Smith & Mark Penta are lifelong friends who met in first grade and attended Catechism school together.

Mark draws. Spencer tries to be funny.